More With Less

More With Less

The Future World of Buckminster Fuller

Nathan Aaseng

Lerner Publications Company • Minneapolis

Dedication: For Charis and Mark and the elusive dream of the dome.

LIBRARY OF CONGRESS CATALOGING-IN-PUBLICATION DATA

Aaseng, Nathan.
    More with less.

    Bibliography: p. 73
    Includes index.
    Summary: A biography of the architect and inventor whose investigations into the principles of nature influenced his designs and helped revolutionize our world.
    1. Fuller, R. Buckminster (Richard Buckminster), 1895-1983 — Juvenile literature. [1. Fuller, R. Buckminster (Richard Buckminster), 1895-1983. 2. Inventors. 3. Architects] I. Title.
TA140.F9A65   1986   620'.0092'4 [B] [92]   86-62
ISBN 0-8225-0498-7 (lib. bdg.)

1 2 3 4 5 6 7 8 9 10 96 95 94 93 92 91 90 89 88 87 86

CONTENTS

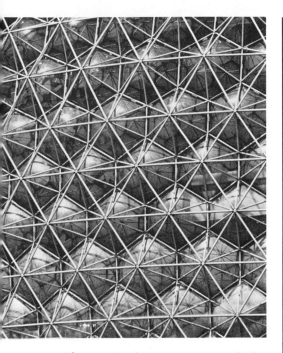

Above: A close-up view of the fantastic structure of a geodesic dome.

This was precisely what Bucky was all about: he knew exactly how to ask all the right and pertinent and searching and devastating questions.
—Peter Blake, editor,
Architectural Forum

INTRODUCTION

Untaught Answers

Remember way back to the time when you used to think that teachers never made mistakes. When you were new to this strange business of school and intensive learning, didn't you marvel at the way your teacher could rattle off answers and explanations to everything without even pausing to think? Maybe you went home awed by these infallible wizards and asked, "How did they get to know all that stuff?"

"They went to school and learned from other teachers," came the answer. But that was more of a stall than an answer, and you weren't going to settle for that. "But who taught those other teachers?" you continued.

"Well, they had to go to school, too, to learn from teachers older than they were." If you weren't so persistent you would have given up and walked away no closer to an answer than when you started. But you kept at it.

"But who taught the *first* teacher?" There you really touched a nerve because you asked something that can't be brushed off with an automatic, one-word answer. Think about all that you've learned over the years and all that's being pumped at you now. Where did it come from? If knowledge were only something handed off from age to age like a bucket in a fire brigade, we'd still be hunting food with crude spears and sleeping on cave floors.

Obviously, something is always being added somewhere in the learning process. Where, then, do the new ideas come from? One way in which they enter our world is through such people as Richard Buckminster Fuller. If you study the life of Bucky Fuller, you may get a clue as to how mankind occasionally breaks through into a world of ideas that no one has dreamed of before. His life may give an inkling of what it was that sparked an ancient mind to use a wheel to lighten the transportation load. Or it may clear up some of the mystery as to how science, medicine, and industry suddenly jumped forward so that the world would be almost unrecognizable to those who died a generation before. His life may make it at least believable that someone could break away

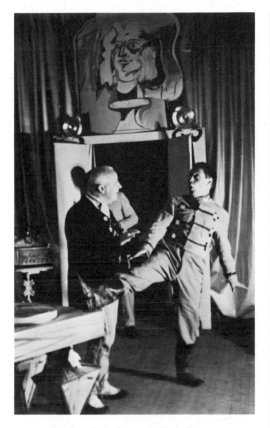

Bucky the show-off, *left*, on stage as Baron Medusa in "The Ruse of the Medusa," August 14, 1948.

not only from popular opinion but from the evidence of his own senses to declare that the world isn't flat, it's round.

So who is Buckminster Fuller? He was a college dropout who failed at one project after another, yet he collected over 2,000 patents in his lifetime. Many have insisted, and continue to insist, that he was a crackpot, a lunatic, a dreamer, a windbag, and a show-off. Others credit him with being a genius, a modern-day Leonardo da Vinci, and the foremost thinker of our time.

How could one person be called all those things at one time? An exercise to help us understand how Fuller's mind worked might also help us understand why his ideas stirred up such heated discussion. Take a look at something we're all familiar with: houses.

The building of houses seems to be one of those things that has improved through the ages. Modern houses are a far cry from dark, damp caves, or flimsy, drafty tents, or the thatched-roof dwellings with the outhouse in the back. The modern version seems to be a pretty good product. It's clean, airtight, energy-efficient. Aluminum siding, landscaped lawns, kitchens full of conveniences, cozy bedrooms, air-conditioning, and wall-to-wall carpeting have all added to our comfort.

Now think about what is still wrong with houses and what we could do to make houses even better. Don't waste time dabbling with the little things like better storm windows or sunken bathtubs. Start over from scratch.

Rethink the whole idea of what kind of covering people ought to live under.

Most of us wouldn't know where to start in redesigning the concept of a house. We probably wouldn't come up with anything much different from what we already have and it likely wouldn't be nearly as good as what many people will be sleeping in tonight. In fact, it seems to be a classic case of "don't fix it if it isn't broken." Why go around trying to dream up new structures to live in when what we have is fine?

Imagine then that you're inviting Buckminster Fuller to inspect your dream house, which is everything you feel a house should be. Bucky would concede that what you have is fine for the present, but wouldn't you like to see into the future, to see a house become something more than what it is now?

Unless you have an extremely unusual house, Fuller could give you four major reasons, without even stepping in the front door, why your house won't hold up against what's coming in the future. He would tell you that your house is:

1. Too restricting: because it's not designed to be moved.
2. Too wasteful of material: because houses don't have to be heavy and massive to be strong.
3. The wrong shape: because it's based on a cube, not a sphere.
4. Too expensive: because it was built on the site rather than at a factory.

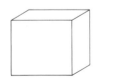

Above: Cube and standard house shape. *Below:* **Sphere and Bucky's geodesic dome.**

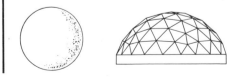

Buckminster Fuller recounting his childhood to an audience at Harvard University Science Center in 1977.

If this list of thoughts had never occurred to you, you're in good company. For decades the housing industry hasn't been able to make sense of them either. And why should they? Fuller's complaints seem so off-the-wall, it's no wonder that so many thought he was out of his mind. Nobody cared how much a house weighed. What difference did it make? In fact, people wanted a heavy house to provide strength, so they wouldn't get blown away by winds like those trailer homes always were. People didn't want houses that moved; if they did, they could buy a tent or trailer. Houses with square corners were solid, easier to build, and could be naturally divided into pleasing, rectangular rooms. Finally, the very idea of prefabricated houses sounded too much like a cheap, disposable house. If you wanted quality you had to pay for it. Didn't it make sense that a house built into the ground, right on the spot, would last longer?

Fuller, however, insisted that his questions were important. The questions led to the invention of spectacular geodesic domes so strong they could stand up to the strongest wind, yet so light they could be transported by helicopter. His ideas of radical new houses were in turn part of a grander scheme. For what Buckminster Fuller really had in mind was a plan to save the human race and lift mankind to a bold new future that overflowed with plenty of everything for everyone in the world.

It's not easy to understand what domes have to do with saving the world. It's hard enough trying to make sense of Fuller's questions, without even getting into the answers! At times, Fuller's brain seemed to be like a satellite which had broken away from all the other satellites in an orbit and went whirring off into space on its own.

How then did Buckminster Fuller break away? How did he come to explore areas that others don't even believe exist? What did he find? Whether you agree with his life or not, the Fuller life was a most unusual adventure.

Octet truss and radome in an exhibit of Buckminster Fuller's designs at the Museum of Modern Art in New York in 1959.

Fuller with his baby sister Rosie at the family's vacation home at Bear Island, Maine.

1
THE SHAPING OF THINGS TO COME

I am not a thing—a noun.
I seem to be a verb—
an evolutionary process—
an integral function of
the universe,
and so are you.
—R.B.F.

Out of Focus

From the time he was born on July 12, 1895, in the Boston suburb of Milton, Massachusetts, Richard Buckminster Fuller saw the world differently from others. At first it was simply a matter of his eyes not working normally. During the first four years of his life, Fuller was slightly cross-eyed and so terribly far-sighted that nothing around him ever came into focus.

While other children explored the clear, sharp boundaries of a table, puzzled over the strange letters of type under the pictures in their books, or marveled at the thousands of distinct leaves that made up a tree, Fuller was seeing something else. Life for him was a mass of blurred images. He could tell the larger ones apart by their general shape and color; smaller images just melted into the background. When he looked at his mother's or father's face, he couldn't see any spark of anger in their eyes or see the corners of their mouths spreading into smiles. A face was just two shadowy shapes on top of a lighter background. Neither he nor his family knew there was anything wrong with him at the time. As far as he knew, everyone saw things the way he did. The world consisted of shapes and patterns, and the trick was to know those patterns well enough to tell one from another.

Fuller's eyesight problems were not even discovered until he reached the age of four. When he was then fitted with corrective glasses, it was as though he had entered an entirely new world. Just as a man dying of thirst sees more in a glass of water than the average person, Bucky marveled at the sights around him. Others his age were already growing numb to "everyday" sights, while Fuller thrilled to the beauty and intricate detail that had suddenly come into focus.

So it was that by the time he reached school age, Bucky had seen the world from

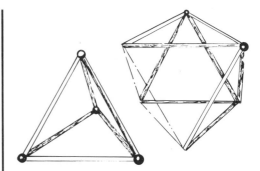

Tetrahedron and octahedron.

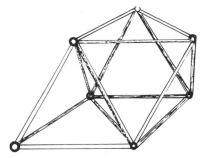

Tetrahedron linked to octahedron in the basic unit of the octet truss.

not one but two angles that are hidden from most of us. He had seen it first as a mysterious swirl of shapes and patterns, and then as a wonderful collection of objects, each as distinct and intriguing as the most elaborate spider web. No one can say how much effect this had on his future ideas. You could put another far-sighted child in the same situation, fit him or her with glasses at age four, and come up with someone who didn't care a bit about shapes.

But Bucky did, and he thought about shapes in a way that no one else had. As early as kindergarten, Fuller showed that he could fashion some breath-taking designs. His teacher passed out dried peas and toothpicks to the class and asked them to create something. No doubt most of the children constructed some kind of house, tower, ball, pole, or just a random mass of toothpicks and peas. Fuller fashioned an odd sculpture, made of alternating octahedrons (eight-sided figures) and tetrahedrons (four-sided figures). This

The spidery lines of the octet truss contrast with the surrounding marble pillars. This exhibit of Fuller's work was set up in the lobby of a bank building in Minneapolis in 1973.

structure later became known as the octet truss. His teacher was awed by the masterpiece, and for good reason. What the five-year-old had designed was so original that, sixty years later, it earned a patent for him. No one could have taught Bucky how to build that shape because, to the best of our knowledge, no one had ever been able to build it before.

Surviving the Schools

Obviously, Buckminster Fuller had a natural talent for new and exciting ideas. One might expect that a good education would be the perfect thing to draw out and direct the best of those thoughts and help Fuller realize his gifts. Unfortunately, despite attending some highly regarded schools, Bucky and his teachers considered themselves lucky just to survive their experiences with each other. It wasn't that the student was not eager to learn. He loved the precision of mathematics and liked to probe into the elements that made up the natural world. The problem came from Fuller's unusual ways of looking at things.

Bucky always bubbled over with questions and he often asked questions that didn't make sense to the average teacher. Rather than accept some of the "given" truths of geometry, for example, Bucky challenged everything.

A page from the patent granted to Bucky on May 30, 1961 for the octet truss.

He pointed out that since "points" were just imaginary places in space and "lines" were just imaginary connections between imaginary points, there really wasn't any such thing as a "plane." After all, how could a plane be real if it was made up of imaginary things?

Questions such as that mattered to Fuller, but they only served to irritate his teachers. It seemed that Bucky insisted on wasting everyone's time on pure foolishness and got side-tracked onto questions that had nothing to do with the lesson at hand. It was particularly frustrating to have this kid constantly challenging statements that generations of students had graciously accepted. How could you go about the teaching process of transferring known facts to someone if that person refused to accept them? Fuller, on the other hand, could not understand what use a school was if you weren't given the freedom to find out the answers you needed to know.

Bucky finally learned that, in school, the best way to *get* along was to *go* along. To keep out of trouble he learned to go along with what the class was doing, even if it didn't always make sense to him. His questions and experiments would have to wait until he could find time to work on them on his own.

As a result, Fuller did well in his studies at Milton Academy and was accepted into one of the nation's most respected colleges, Harvard University. Again, however, the combination of a top school with a brilliant mind only caused misery. This time social problems

Milton Academy, the private prep school Fuller attended. Most of the students boarded at the school, but Bucky was a day student and lived at home.

were piled onto the classroom clashes. Bucky was a sensitive young man who wanted very much to fit in with the group. Yet everything about him guaranteed that he would be an outsider among the students at Harvard. His father had died when Bucky was thirteen, leaving the family much poorer than the families of the other boys at Harvard. His unusual ideas and his overly enthusiastic personality also caused classmates to avoid him. Lonely and depressed, Bucky neglected his studies. He then wasted what money he had on a wild party trip to New York, and he was expelled before completing one year. After being sent by his angry family to work in a Canadian textile mill, Bucky seemed to have straightened himself out, and he was welcomed back to Harvard. But he again found it so uninteresting that he was asked to leave a second time.

It seemed that Fuller had blown his chance to develop his brilliant talents. How far could a person go in the world of ideas when he couldn't even handle a college course? The disturbing answer Fuller gave was that his lack of formal classroom education was a blessing. Fuller criticized schools as being too restricting. They tried to harness and "discipline" the mind rather than giving it room to grow. To him, courses were too specialized and were taught as if they had nothing to do with each other. The barrage of facts tended to clutter the mind instead of clearing it for new ideas. During one stage of his life, Fuller

Buckminster Fuller, Harvard man.

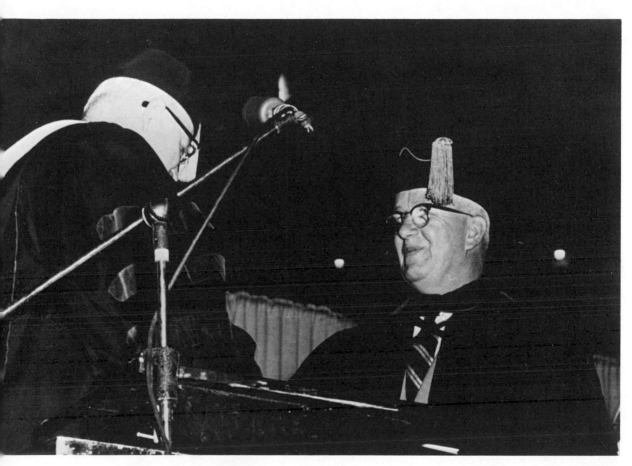

Above: Fuller received his first honorary college degree, the degree of Doctor of Design, from North Carolina State College of Agriculture and Engineering on June 6, 1954. Although he never did graduate from college, he received over 40 honorary degrees, including one from Oxford University in England.

decided that he actually needed to unlearn much of what he had been taught in school. He went nearly two years without speaking to anyone—except, on occasion, to his wife and daughter—in hopes that he could break himself of all the bad habits of thought and speech that he had picked up in his years of schooling. To his dying day, Buckminster Fuller looked forward to the day when the "schoolhouse" would disappear.

Looking for a Better Way

Fuller never did complete a college education. His attitude toward the educational system left him more than ever an outsider, free to work out his own strange ideas without any peer pressure. Being an outsider can sometimes be an advantage, especially when it comes to inventing. Instead of trying to master known ways of doing things, Bucky liked to tinker with new and better ways of doing those same things.

An early example of this happened at his family's Bear Island vacation spot in Maine. The island was quite remote and it was Bucky's job to row the two miles to Eagle Island to pick up the family mail. Being stocky, strong, and a willing worker, Fuller didn't mind putting his muscles to work. What bothered him was that he had to face backwards when he rowed. That meant that he had to keep looking over his shoulder to check if he was staying on course. During a thick fog, a person could be driven dizzy twisting his or her neck every couple of strokes to look ahead.

Most of us would accept that as a fact of rowing and satisfy ourselves by grumbling about it. Bucky, though, was not good at accepting "facts." There had to be a way to make the job easier. He couldn't do much about the foggy conditions, so he looked for a way to change the rowing process. An experienced observer of the world, Fuller remem-

The Fuller family at their Bear Island vacation home. *Left to right*, Bucky, his sister Rosie, his mother, his father, and his brother Woolcott.

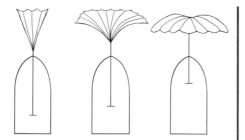

The improved rowboat. *Left*, the umbrella is closed and at rest. *Center*, it is partly opened, and is beginning to pull water toward the boat. *Right*, the umbrella has been pushed open.

Bucky loved the water all his life.

bered how a jellyfish propels itself through the water, sort of like an umbrella opening and collapsing. Maybe that would work with a row boat. Fuller rigged what looked like an inverse umbrella to the front of his boat. When he pushed his lever, the umbrella would open, forcing water toward the boat and moving the craft forward. When he pulled on it, the umbrella would collapse, ready to start another stroke. Not only did Bucky's invention work, saving wear and tear on his neck, it got him across the water in half the time it had taken him to row.

Years later, Fuller was back on the seas, patrolling the Atlantic Coast during World War I. One of his duties was to be alert to the Navy planes which practiced their landings on the water in his area. During these training sessions, pilots occasionally approached the sea at too steep an angle. The front of the pontoons would catch in the water, causing the plane to flip over. Although the boats raced to the rescue, the planes quickly filled with water, sometimes trapping and drowning the stunned pilot.

Fuller could not bear the thought of a man drowning while the rescuers fumbled frantically to get him out. He designed a crane-like instrument that could be attached to his boat and could quickly flip the plane back to its right position. During its first try, the device saved enough time that they were able to save the pilot's life.

Bucky's work for the Navy did not go

unnoticed. He received a promotion and a chance to study in the Navy's engineering school. This was a different and more enjoyable educational experience for Fuller. He was fascinated by propellers and turbines and the principles that made them work. The Navy also impressed him with its efficiency: wasted space and weight were trimmed from a warship to give it the most equipment at the least sacrifice of speed and maneuverability. Bucky studied the most modern equipment and inventions such as the wireless radio. He looked at the way ships were designed to slide through the *water* with the least resistance, and sought out the most efficient design for cutting the *wind* resistance of land vehicles. All of his studies seemed to point toward a single goal of invention: getting more with less.

For the rest of his life, Buckminster Fuller insisted that this was the key principle in improving the world. Ways had to be found to increase production or benefits using less work and material. He would carry his argument to its extreme, saying that unemployment was not a bad thing. In fact, he thought the goal of a society should be 100% unemployment. In other words, a society should be able to find ways to give its people what they needed without requiring that they put in time at jobs: more with less.

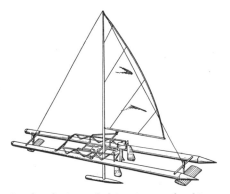

Bucky designed this strange-looking boat on needle-shaped pontoons or floats. An example of his "more with less" philosophy, it is more stable and efficient and uses less material than standard boats.

The *Inca*, the boat which Fuller commanded when rescuing crashed Navy pilots.

Bubbles and the Secrets of the Universe

While in the Navy, Bucky had formulated his goal: making more with less. But unless he wanted to spend his life blindly tinkering with whatever suited his fancy, he needed to come up with a plan. How could he *best* go about reaching his goal?

Once again Bucky discovered an important answer on the deck of a ship. While staring at the swirling froth kicked up by the ship, Fuller began to focus on the millions of tiny bubbles that made up the froth. Most of us have watched the bubbles in foam many times with a certain fascination, but have probably not thought much about them. But Bucky's long-standing curiosity about shapes drew him to look more closely at those tiny bubbles. Each of them appeared to be a perfectly shaped sphere. Thinking of spheres, Fuller recalled the familiar mathematical number called pi (π), that everyone uses when working with the dimensions of a sphere. Who but an outsider like Buckminster Fuller would dare challenge the reality of pi?

But there was something about pi that didn't fit in with what he was seeing. Pi is an irrational number. You can compute it to however many places you have time for and never get it to the end, never find out exactly what pi is. You can call it 3.14 or 3.14159 or any number of places beyond. The pi that you use in figuring can never be anything more than a rounded-off number or, in Bucky's words, a guess. But the bubbles he was seeing appeared to be perfect spheres. Mankind had created this artificial number, pi, to help describe and think about bubbles and spheres. Using pi, they thought they knew what a sphere was, what its dimensions were and how to describe it. But nature ignores mankind's geometry and makes *perfect* spheres. Nature does not use a rounded-off estimate of number to make a sphere: every bubble is perfect, not an approximate sphere. Bucky thought that maybe pi doesn't really describe what a bubble is or how it's made. Maybe we should throw out that sloppy, artificial tool for looking at spheres, and look at them again.

That wasn't all that the young Navy man saw in those bubbles. He also saw that it was tension and compression that caused the bubble to take and hold its shape. The air inside pushed against the water around it, and the water stuck together and compressed the air inside it. Fuller saw this as an example of a balance of two forces, one pushing in and one pushing out. It struck him that this kind of balance would be the most efficient way to lend strength to a structure.

Excitedly, Bucky concluded that the secrets of making more with less were hidden in nature. If he could begin to figure out how the universe was set up, he could make huge strides in making more with less. One of the basic questions he explored had to do with his special interest in shapes. What were the

Bucky's interest in the forces of tension and compression led to the development of "tensegrity" figures. *Left*: One of his students at Southern Illinois University in the late 1950s holds a tensegrity sphere. *Below*: Fuller holds a smaller model of the tensegrity sphere. Straight sticks and tight wires form a model of the forces in a bubble. The sticks push out but the wires pull in, and although the sticks don't touch each other the sphere holds its shape.

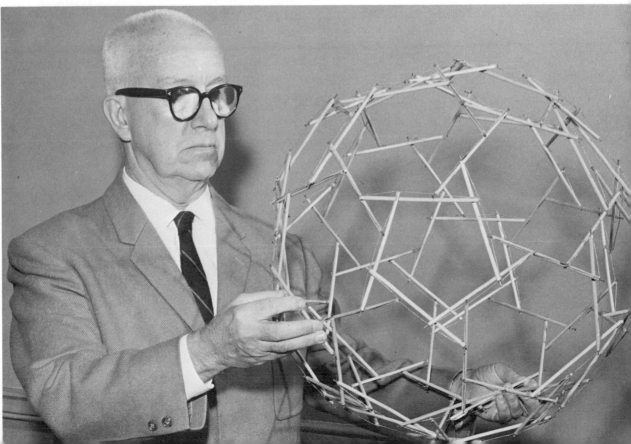

simplest shapes and forms that nature used in making more complex figures? Was there in fact one basic form that was more stable than all other forms? In his efforts to find out, Fuller went back to that old kindergarten activity of building with blocks and balls. He would play games such as seeing how many spheres could be packed closely around a central sphere, and then ponder whether or not that number had some special meaning in nature. Were these somehow the numbers that the universe is based on? Were these shapes the basic building blocks of nature?

Drawings of close-packing of spheres. *Top:* Twelve spheres surround one sphere. All touch their neighbors. *Bottom:* The same basic shape with more layers of spheres added. Fuller's interest in the basic shapes and numbers of nature led him to develop a new geometry, *Synergetics,* based not on imaginary lines but on real, buildable models such as these.

Tragedy, or, Design Science

This kind of off-in-the-stars thinking might have been just a brain-teasing exercise except that Bucky was jolted by a very real human event. Bucky had married Anne Hewlett in 1917 and a year and a half later the Fullers had a baby girl, whom they named Alexandra. Far from being a cold, distant intellectual, Fuller was an affectionate man who was even prouder than most fathers of his little girl. Bucky was still "in love with the world" and having a daughter around made it twice as much fun. He could experience again the newness of that world that he had discovered with his first pair of glasses. It tickled him to watch a little person learn through discovery,

Anne Hewlett Fuller and Buckminster Fuller in their dome home at Carbondale, Illinois around 1967.

through feeling, tasting, and seeing things she had never met before.

The happy moments, though, were often crowded out by anxious ones. Alexandra could not stay healthy and she contracted one serious illness after another. When the Fullers finally nursed her through a critical case of flu, she came down with spinal meningitis. Sparing no expense, they desperately sought out the best care they could give her. But despite everything they did, they could not prevent pneumonia from setting in. Bucky's world was shattered when he had to bury his first-born child; she was just about the age he had been when the beauty of the world had first opened up to him.

In all his years, Fuller could never push the tragedy very far from his thoughts. Fifty years later he still spoke of the helplessness he felt as they lost their girl. What grated on him the worst was that it could so easily have been prevented. As years went by, more and more diseases were eliminated from everyday life: cures were discovered, ways of prevention developed. With more effort and planning, these scientific discoveries could have been made sooner.

Advancing the cause of science became an urgent project for Fuller. If future discoveries had come sooner in medical research, his Alexandra might have lived. So it was that Buckminster Fuller zeroed in on the future. Along with making more with less, Fuller saw the need to plan for the future in order to take advantage of the least bit of scientific progress. As a result, he developed his theory of design science. The key to this theory was control. Mankind must be able to master its environment in order to solve its problems. He believed that you can't change people for the better without changing their environment for the better. That would take careful planning. As far as Bucky could tell, society never planned for the future. Most solutions to problems were like aspirin: they made the problem go away for a while but didn't cure it. Fuller insisted we should not fight and then grudgingly accept change, but should be a step ahead and ready for change before it came.

Dymaxion Failures

With the help of a public relations person, Fuller coined a name for his efforts to produce more with less: Dymaxion. The name was a combination of two words that Fuller liked to use: "dynamic" and "maximum," with another scientific-sounding word, "ion," thrown in at the end.

Among his early ideas were a Dymaxion house and a Dymaxion car. The Dymaxion house was to have no wasted space and was to have its own built-in systems so it wouldn't be tied to sewer and water pipelines. Bucky designed one that was portable and actually used the sun's energy to create a flow of air that cooled it. The bathroom could provide all the usual services, including shower (still a new idea to most people at that time), with just a few gallons of water—which could be recycled. Fuller worked throughout the 1930s to design a reasonably-priced Dymaxion

Fuller's sketch of the Dymaxion car from the patent issued in 1937. This is the top and side view.

Above: The standard automobile in 1932 was about as "aerodynamic" as the horse-drawn wagon it had replaced. Its box shape pushed through the air inefficiently. *Below:* Fuller's Dymaxion car. Bucky studied the flow of air around moving objects to find the most efficient shape for the car.

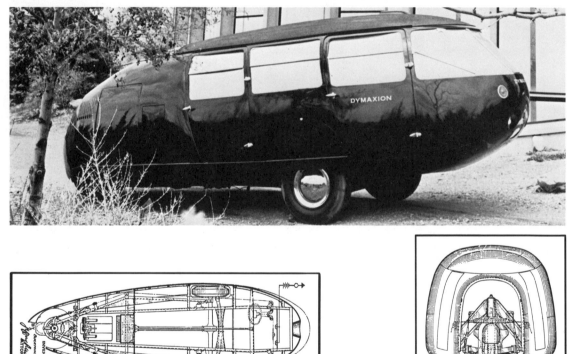

Left: A drawing from the Dymaxion car patent shows the arrangement of the three wheels. The two in front provided power, the one in back was for steering. *Right:* The car viewed from the back. The skin of the car was a smooth, continuous curve, much like the hull of a boat.

Patent number 2,101,057, for the Dymaxion car. Fuller never patented the Dymaxion house. It was the first invention he tried to patent by himself, and the Patent Office rejected his application. He later found out that a first rejection from the Patent Office was really a request to rewrite the application, but he never reapplied for the Dymaxion house patent.

Dwelling Machine in an effort to make it a permanent part of America's housing scene, and finally produced two prototypes in 1944-45. Being an outsider to the establishment presented serious problems to Fuller, though. Architects were furious that a man who had no training at all in architecture would try to tell them how houses ought to be built. Their ridicule, as well as the public's built-in suspicion of anything too new, doomed his first efforts at Dymaxion structures.

The same thing happened to his Dymaxion car, which came out in 1933. Leaving behind all fashionable ideas of what a car should be, Fuller came up with a streamlined design modeled after an airplane body. Bucky's car could hold eleven passengers comfortably and offered excellent visibility for driver and passengers. Perhaps the car's oddest feature was its wheel placement. The car had two wheels in front but only one in back. This made it so easy to handle that Fuller once circled a policeman in it, with the front of the car never more than inches away from the officer during his circle. Parallel parking headaches were eliminated with the car. All a person had to do was head straight into the parking space and then swing the tail around to the curb. Unfortunately, any chance that Bucky's design had of catching on was destroyed when one of his three Dymaxion cars was involved in a fatal collision. Although the other driver, operating a standard car, was at fault, news reports of the crash made it sound as if Fuller's invention was a death trap. The bad publicity guaranteed that no one would spend a cent to help him produce his revolutionary design.

The Brink of Suicide

By 1927 all the ingredients were there for Buckminster Fuller to stun the world with his genius. The energy, the ideas, and the theories for some bold new plans were all in place. Yet at the same time, Fuller was drawing dangerously close to suicide. Ironically, the man with the bright vision of the future could see no future for himself. Fuller had been a failure by almost any definition of the business world. He had failed in college. He had moved from the East Coast to a strange city, Chicago, only to be fired from an important job as head of a growing company. His ideas were scoffed at, he had no way to support his family, and no money for any of his projects. The harder he tried, it seemed, the worse he failed.

For a sensitive man like Bucky, it was too much to take. One night he wandered over to Lake Michigan with thoughts of drowning himself. Before taking the final step toward suicide, though, he had one last talk with himself on the shores. He could comfort himself with arguments such as that his wife and his new daughter Allegra would be taken care of by his family much better than by him, the failure. But fortunately, Fuller's mind could wander off to probe the universe even in a life-or-death situation. As he thought of the world and how he fit into it, he decided that he had no right to take his own life. He had unique experiences, ideas, and knowledge to offer to others. He was a part of the universe; in fact, he went so far as to say that he *belonged* to the universe.

That thought was so powerful it not only roused him from depression, it had him bubbling over with enough energy to see him through two more decades of frustration and ridicule. Bucky had finally found a mission to match his inventiveness. He wasn't working for a company or a boss, or even for himself; he was working for the universe. Buckminster Fuller was determined to hunt for ways to plan for the future, to make more with less, to work for the well-being of people everywhere.

Rather than rush right out and get started, as one might expect from someone as strong-willed as he, Bucky stopped dead in his tracks. He decided his mission was so important that he needed to clear his mind and start fresh. For two years the Fuller family scraped by, living in Chicago in a slum while Bucky did nothing but think. Those were the two years he refused to speak, for fear that the speech patterns he had learned over the years would get in the way of his thought. Accountable to

Fuller in his office at Southern Illinois University in the 1960s—still thinking.

no one, Fuller freed his mind so that it could explore and wrestle with all the questions he could think of. At long last, we finally meet a Buckminster Fuller who is capable of stunning the architectural world with his spectacular geodesic domes.

A spectacular example of the geodesic dome.

Above: Architect's drawing of a geodesic dome home.

Fuller, for a long time, was considered a kind of H. G. Wells of housing. You either read him for amusement or just didn't pay attention.
— William Marlin, editor,
Architectural Forum

2
DOMES

Battling an Old Enemy —Tradition

Fuller should have known better than to tinker with the housing industry. Together with his father-in-law, James Monroe Hewlett, he had once tried to breathe some fresh air into the construction business. Mr. Hewlett had developed a new brick, made of a fibrous material like straw, with holes in the center of it. In 1923 he hired Bucky to get a business going to produce the bricks. One of the unique advantages of the Stockade Building System's new product was that the holes in the bricks could be lined up one on top of another and concrete poured down into the holes to form a solid support. The bricks even made a layer of insulation inside the walls unnecessary. The Stockade system made construction less expensive and less wasteful, and fewer skilled workers were needed to build houses with this system. During the four years that Fuller worked for Stockade, the company helped build 240 houses. Unfortunately, neither Bucky nor his father-in-law made the fortune they expected.

Their problems in the business, which forced Mr. Hewlett to sell out his share of the company and got Bucky fired, gave Fuller a painful, close-up look at a tradition-bound industry. He concluded that architects weren't much different from car designers in Detroit or fashion experts in Paris. All of them spent their time designing different "looks" without making any real changes. People in the 1930s and 1940s were still building houses basically the same way they built them a hundred years ago. Fuller scoffed that much of the technology used in house-building hadn't changed in over a thousand years. Even if the architects would accept a new idea, the construction workers would object because they might have to learn new methods or fewer of them might be needed for a job. Fuller continued to search for a breakthrough that would bring home construction into the 20th century. But

The Stockade Brick Building System. *Above:* A single brick. *Below:* A portion of a wall built according to Hewlett's system, with part cut away to show the columns of concrete which form when the holes in the bricks are lined up.

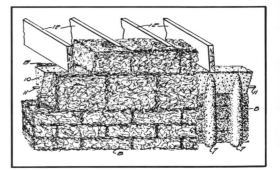

his Dymaxion houses of the 1930s only struck people as bizarre. In fact, his only success at the time was due to the fact that a Chicago department store considered them something out of the future. A couple of Bucky's houses were ordered as a background to set off a display of futuristic furniture. The rest of his experiments were ignored or rejected.

Fuller, however, was convinced he was onto something. The only thing that could stop him was lack of money. With some gifts from friends and supporters, Fuller kept at his revolutionary housing plans. He saw the current building process as terribly expensive, wasteful and confining. Fuller saw four new questions which defined the ideal housing he wanted to design.

Can it be easily moved?

When he was younger, Bucky used to admire the enormous floating airships called dirigibles. They were as large as houses yet could sail anywhere in the world. When Bucky looked at history, he saw that some of the world's greatest advances involved making people more mobile. Trains, automobiles, and airplanes rushed people to points all over the globe. Electronic radio and telephone allowed voices to travel even farther in less time. Why not, then, continue in that direction and pry houses loose from the soil? Bucky could not understand why anyone would want to tie himself and all his possessions to a tiny plot of land. Far better to build a house that could be carried with you wherever you wished to go.

How much does it weigh?

This question comes out of the first because, obviously, a house that is going to be moved should weigh as little as possible. In the construction industry, though, weight was considered a good thing, if it was even considered at all. Weight was what held most buildings together; the force of pressure (compression) from above kept the lower pieces in place. When you thought of a good, solid structure, one that would last beyond a century, you thought of massive granite pillars.

Bucky believed this was all nonsense. Remembering the forces in a bubble and a dirigible, he proposed that a house could be made strong by using the force of tension instead of compression. He believed in building a house in such a way that powerful forces

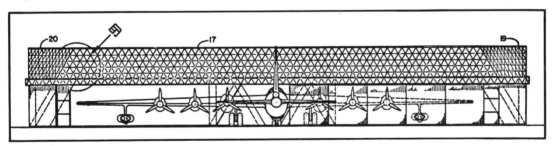

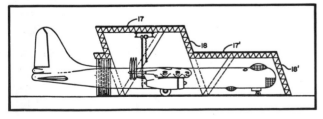

The octet truss is an example of the efficient use of tension. In his patent application Bucky sketched a plane hangar built of the octet truss. The web of struts spreads the stress so no supporting walls or columns are needed inside.

would pull outward and these would be perfectly balanced by the forces that held the material together. Not only would this building be stronger than a house that relied on gravity to hold it together, it would also be much less wasteful. Thousands of pounds of brick, stone, and wood could be trimmed from a house and put to better use. Building a better house with only a fraction of the material perfectly met Bucky's philosophy of more with less.

What shape is it?

Cube-shaped houses have become so common that it is hard to imagine a modern house based on another shape. Ask any child to draw a house and almost certainly he or she will draw a box shape. Fuller's studies had shown him, though, that a rectangle was not the ideal shape on which to base a building.

His probings of shapes and of the key building blocks of the universe had led him to favor the triangle. The triangle had to be the basic shape of the universe because it was the only shape that could not be divided into something smaller. Cut a square in half and what do you get? Two triangles. Cut a triangle in half and what do you get? Two triangles. Bucky then concluded that there was no stability of form except in triangles. He pointed out that even builders of rectangular houses ought to know this. For how did a builder add stability to his rectangular structure? With diagonal supports, which, in effect, reduced a rectangle to two triangles.

Of course Bucky didn't like to deal only in two dimensions, so he went on to conclude that it was the tetrahedron that was actually the basic shape of the universe. Theoretically, then, the most stable, economical way to go was to build pyramids.

The problem with tetrahedral houses, aside from the fact that any architect who proposed them would get laughed all the way to Egypt, was that they couldn't make good use of the forces of tension needed to make a light, strong structure. For that, you had to borrow the shape of the bubble, a sphere. Fuller certainly wasn't going to argue that people

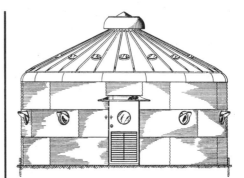

Fuller designed a house built from a grain silo. The "Dymaxion Deployment Unit" was mass-producible because it could be made in the same fashion as a grain silo and installed anywhere.

should live inside balls, but an automobile trip through the heartland of the Midwest helped him to zero in on how the sphere could be used to make a practical dwelling. Simply, he took a close look at another sight that most of us have brushed off a hundred times, a farm storage bin or silo. A silo was basically a sphere cut in half on top of a cylinder. It was sturdy even without any internal supports. Cylinders, Bucky knew, contained more useful space on less ground than cubes. Fuller decided then that a half sphere or a *dome* was worth looking at. It could allow more room on less area *and* use the tension properties of the sphere to make a stronger house with less material.

The idea of constructing with domes was nothing new. Some of the earliest human dwellings were dome-shaped. Domes have been used throughout the world, from the ice igloos of Arctic peoples to the Zulu kraals of South Africa to the beautiful tombs of the ancient Greeks. They have proven their durability time and again. The most striking example came out of the ashes of the horrible bombing of Hiroshima. The atomic bomb that in 1945 devastated buildings for miles around left only a single structure standing amid the rubble. It was no coincidence that the surviving building was dome-shaped. What Fuller did was not to come up with a radical new shape, but to find convincing reasons why the 20th century should *progress* to where we were thousands of years ago.

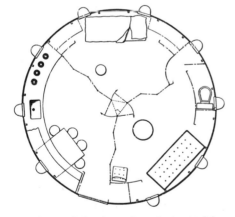

A view of the interior. A movable curtain could divide the building into three rooms: bedroom (top), living room (the bathroom is in this area), and kitchen (bottom left).

Where does the construction take place?

You would hardly think that it would be a difficult task to talk people into saving money. But Buckminster was scorched by some of his most heated opposition on this point.

Fuller would argue his case by asking you to imagine that you wanted to buy a new car. Suppose that you first hired a person to sit down and draw careful blueprints of what your car should look like and how it should be built. Next you would hire a contractor to oversee the project. Trucks would deliver sheet metal, glass, plastic, electrical equipment, engine parts, etc., to your driveway. Then subcontractors would come in and take their turns at their various specialties. Doors would be cut to the correct size. Upholsterers would come in to get the seats covered and the carpeting installed. Glassworkers would cut windows to size and install them, mechanics would put together the engine and install that. Painters and electricians would come in to do their specialties.

The whole scene, of course, is ridiculous. Cars built that way would cost a fortune, and very few people could afford them. The only reason that cars are practical for the average American today is that they are produced on an assembly line. Advances in mass production techniques allow many cars to be made quite quickly in one spot, the factory.

Buckminster Fuller wanted to know why houses should be treated differently. Why should they be constructed by hand, on the

A prosperous and satisfied Bucky around 1946. He had worked on several projects for the government during the war, including the Dymaxion Deployment Unit, and was just beginning to work out the idea of the geodesic dome.

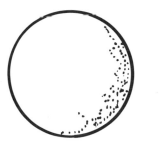

Sphere: the most volume that could be contained with the least surface material. The strongest form against internal pressure.

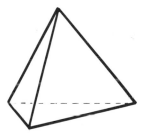

Tetrahedron: the least volume that could be contained with the most surface material, but the strongest form against external pressure, and the most stable structure.

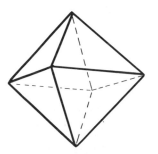

Octahedron: the start of a compromise.

site, when it could be done for a fraction of the cost by mass production techniques at a factory? As far as he could see, the construction industry had all kinds of advanced technology available to help it boost its efficiency. Instead it continued to send out individuals to measure and cut and piece together materials just as they had done for hundreds of years. Fuller insisted that we needed a way of mass-producing houses to provide plentiful, inexpensive housing for the world.

Out of these questions came a basic plan to revolutionize the construction industry. Fuller wanted to mass-produce parts to construct a sturdy, stable, light-weight house. The building should be easy to assemble, movable, and inexpensive. In order to achieve this, he believed the shape of the structure ought to include the virtues of a sphere (a dome): strength against internal pressures, and the economical use of space. But at the same time it would be nice if it could also include the virtues of a triangle: stability, or strength against external pressures. If ever there was a case of trying to have your cake and eat it too, this seemed to be it. How could a building be both a triangle and a sphere at the same time? It seemed that Buckminster Fuller was going to have to choose one or the other.

The Geodesic Dome

Inventors and creative persons often claim to come up with their best ideas while in bed, while shaving, or while busy at any number of things that have nothing to do with their work. So it was that Fuller bumped into a solution to one problem while working on another. This time the focus of attention was a map.

The map project was another offshoot of his fascination for shapes. The challenge was to make a flat, rectangular map that *accurately* displayed a spherical world. The problem is best illustrated by those rectangular maps which stretch the longitudinal and latitudinal

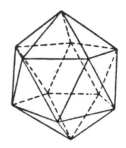

Icosahedron, a 20-sided figure. The step between an octahedron and a sphere.

The most common world map. The further from the equator, the greater the amount of error. Note the relative sizes of Greenland and South America.

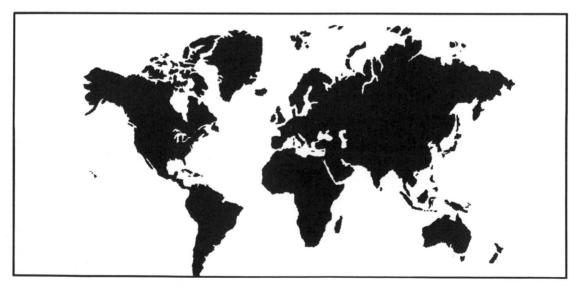

Icosahedron exploded onto a sphere. Each line forms a great circle, the largest circle that can be drawn on the surface of a sphere.

lines that converge near the poles so that Greenland appears to be larger than South America. For centuries mapmakers had puzzled how to flatten the globe onto a piece of paper without creating severe distortion.

Fuller solved the mystery with his Dymaxion Map. He divided the world into carefully calculated rectangles and triangles on a flat surface. With the proper folds along the sides of each triangle or rectangle, the flat map could actually be made into a roughly spherical shape.

Bucky used the same approach in working on a sphere made up of triangles. This led him to develop the *geodesic* dome, the one idea among all the rest that would make him

Fuller's Dymaxion Airocean World Map, the first and only map patented by the U.S. Patent Office. Note the relative sizes of Greenland and South America.

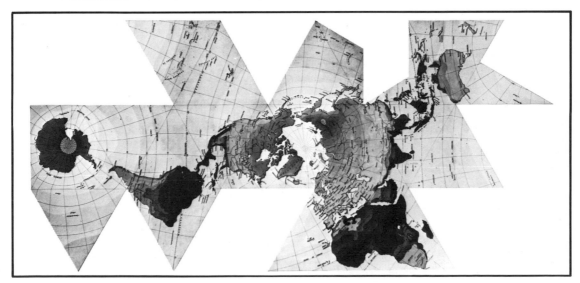

famous. A geodesic on a sphere is defined as the shortest line between two points on the sphere. The dome that Bucky created was given that name because its shape is formed by the careful construction of a large number of geodesics.

Fuller found that by inscribing 31 great circles on a sphere (the equator is an example of a great circle) he could divide the sphere's surface into triangles. There was his combination of sphere and triangle! Bucky was thrilled. The triangles would give maximum strength with a minimum surface because the

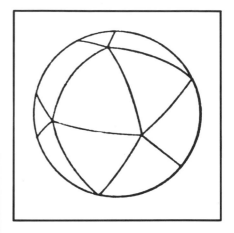

The great circles on the sphere are combined and simplified into triangles on the sphere.

Fuller in his studio about 1950. A great circle dome hangs in the upper left and a geodesic dome is on the floor behind Bucky.

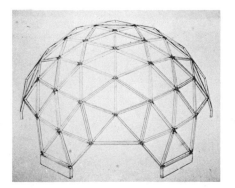

A simple version of a geodesic dome shows how stresses are distributed throughout the interlocking pentagons and hexagons.

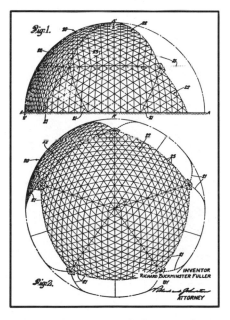

Patent drawings of the geodesic dome.

stress would be distributed evenly at all points. The strength of each section was boosted because it could distribute whatever stress was placed on it to other sections. An illustration of how this works can be seen simply in the different shapes that occur within the sphere. A side of a triangle may at the same time be a side of a larger pentagon (five-sided figure). A corner of a large pentagon is also the center of a hexagon (six-sided figure) and the corner of a different hexagon. Whereas a rectangular building may be only as strong as its weakest link, this geodesic dome could withstand a high wind or earthquake because the entire structure would work together against the destructive force.

It's one thing to say that it is possible to build an incredibly strong, lightweight dome out of triangles, and quite another to actually build one. After the long run of bad luck that had plagued his projects, Bucky was able to benefit from at least one good break. The ancient Greeks had known about geodesic spheres. Their most available building material, however, was rock. Since it would not have worked to build a geodesic dome out of stones, their knowledge was tucked into a forgotten corner. It was Bucky's fortune to come out with his theories on lightweight structures at a time when new building materials were being discovered that could actually make his dreams possible. Aluminum alloys could provide strong, lightweight support, resistant vinyl could be stretched over it for a durable, yet almost transparent skin, and new foam materials could add insulation without adding a great deal of weight.

All that then stood in the way of building his geodesic dome was a marathon of calculating. Accuracy was crucial to the success of his dome. Most construction projects could give or take an eighth of an inch on their measurements and come out all right. But in order for Fuller's dome to work out, each piece had to be within five-thousandths (.005) of an inch of the target. Fuller's timing with building materials was great but he just missed out on the benefits of a computer. From 1947 to 1948, he kept busy working out all the mathematics for his science of geodesics. Bucky was so enthusiastic about his work that he didn't want to take the time for a good night's sleep. He found that he could use his time much better if he took a short nap when he first felt tired rather than waiting until the end of the day for a deep sleep. It was not unusual for him to go for weeks on a pattern of six hours of work followed by a half hour rest, six hours work, a half-hour rest, etc.

In 1948 Buckminster went to Black Mountain College in North Carolina, to try and turn dreams and calculations into reality. Black Mountain was not the average college; instead it was sort of a loose gathering place for people with a passion for education. Backed by a $30,000 gift that had come about from one of Anne Fuller's investments, Bucky

labored hard at getting his first geodesic dome ready for public display.

Before a small crowd of well-wishers, Fuller made his first attempt at raising his dome. The thing collapsed almost immediately. A true scientist, Fuller claimed that this first dome was a test of his ideas, from which he had learned a great deal.

Later that year, though, Bucky finally produced his geodesic dome. At last he had proof that it was possible to build a sturdy, mobile, lightweight building. Fuller's dome, 14 feet in diameter, could be packed and transported in a station wagon. A few of the architects who had hooted at Fuller's ideas over the years were impressed. There were even some nibbles of interest in his dome. In 1949 the Pentagon asked Fuller for a model of his invention. The next year, Fuller was able to construct a 50-foot dome in Montreal, Canada.

Success!

The big break came in 1952. The Ford Motor Company was celebrating its 50th anniversary and the head of the company, Henry Ford II, had a bold plan for making it a memorable occasion. He remembered that his father, founder of the company, had dreamed of building a dome over the courtyard at their Dearborn, Michigan plant. After con-

At Black Mountain College, Bucky took time to have a little fun. He appeared in a play, *left*, with William Shrauger, *right*, with Elaine de Kooning.

The Ford rotunda.

The outline of St. Peter's in Rome, compared with an 800-foot geodesic dome. The dome of St. Peter's, spanning 137½ feet, weighs 10,000 tons by itself. The 800-foot geodesic dome would weigh a total of only 1,000 tons.

sulting with experts, Ford realized that he was probably asking too much. The least they could get by with was a 93-foot dome. A conventional steel dome of that size would weigh about 160 tons and there just was not enough structural support to hold up that much weight.

Buckminster Fuller's reputation had been slowly spreading, though, and it was suggested that they listen to his ideas before giving up on the project. The company's board of directors must have swallowed hard when an enthusiastic Fuller came in with a proposal.

50

Bucky claimed that he could design a dome for them that would weigh only eight and a half tons, and he wouldn't even need a crane to do the job. Some of the directors must have heard how Fuller had been ridiculed in the past, and his wild claim of an eight-and-a-half ton dome must have made them even more suspicious of this character. That was twenty times lighter than a conventional dome. Several of the directors wanted nothing to do with Bucky.

But Fuller was given a chance to show what he could do. Despite having no experience in a large-scale project such as this, Bucky completed his dome (eight and a half tons, as he had promised) on schedule. The effect was better than Ford could have dreamed. Visitors to the courtyard gaped in awe at the fascinating webwork of Bucky's "octet truss" pattern towering above them.

On June 29, 1954, patent #2,682,235 was awarded to R. Buckminster Fuller. At last one of Fuller's ideas, "a way of enclosing space," had become a phenomenal success. The success of the Ford venture sparked new interest in Bucky's domes, and the exclusive rights to the structure given him by the patent assured a steady flow of money for the first time in his career.

The United States Department of Defense came calling, asking whether Fuller's domes could stand up to rugged polar conditions. Their plans were to set up a 4,500-mile-long Distant Early Warning (DEW) line along the

Patent #2,682,235.

The "radome" Bucky designed for the DEW line.

Arctic Circle to detect any missiles that might be heading for the United States. Listening to their requirements, Fuller knew that his domes would be put to the most severe test. Materials would have to be light enough so that planes could deliver them to inaccessible areas. Brutal weather conditions made it important that the building be constructed *very* quickly, yet be strong enough to stand up to winds whipping around at 200 miles per hour. Finally, because it interfered with the short-wave tracking signals of the radar equipment the domes would house, metal could not be used in the structures. Fuller's "radomes" did the trick. Fourteen hours after the pieces were unloaded from the plane, the 40-foot-high domes were up and working.

There seemed to be no end to the needs that this strange structure could meet. The United States Marines came closest to matching Buckminster Fuller's original intentions

The dome in Hawaii. This was the first dome built by the Kaiser Aluminum Company, and president Henry Kaiser wanted to watch it go up. He caught a plane from San Francisco the day workmen started building the dome, but by the time he arrived in Honolulu it was already finished.

when they asked for domes to serve as temporary shelters. The domes they received could be picked up by helicopters and flown intact to a new location. Bucky's transportable house was now a reality!

In 1957 a geodesic dome was chosen to house a concert hall in Hawaii. The materials were flown in and less than 24 hours after they were unpacked, the building was filled with over 1,800 concert goers. It had taken less than a day to construct a large (145 feet in diameter) dome which provided the musical director with the best acoustics he had ever experienced.

Domes began to pop up in all sizes for widely different purposes. In 1957 smaller domes were mass-produced, ready to compete with swings and slides for children's attention on the playground. A year later, a massive dome was taking shape in Baton Rouge, Louisiana. The resulting cavern, 384 feet in diameter and 128 feet high, provided shelter for workers to rebuild a whole train of railroad cars at one time.

The hottest demand for Fuller's new dome was at fairs around the world. American exhibitors recognized Bucky's achievement as a uniquely American contribution to architecture and they were proud to set up shop under the new domes. By the late 1950s

Geodesic playdome.

The dome in Baton Rouge for the Union Tank Car Company.

Bucky outside the dome at the Moscow World's Fair.

Below: **Nikita Khruschchev and then-Vice President Richard Nixon outside the dome in Moscow.**

these strange honeycombed structures were appearing around the world. At the 1956 Kabul Trade Fair in Afghanistan, workers putting together pavilions for other countries were puzzled by the arrival of a planeload of metal bars. Within two days, untrained laborers had bolted together a dome 135 feet across and 100 feet high. Bucky's geodesic dome, using only paper for its skin, won the Grand Prize at the Tenth International Design Fair in Milan, Italy. A 200-foot diameter dome captured most of the attention at the 1959 Moscow World's Fair. Soviet Union leader Nikita Khrushchev was more than impressed. "I want Mr. J. Buckingham Fuller to come to the Soviet Union to teach our engineers," he said. Buckminster Fuller shrugged off the butchering of his name and often did visit Russia to offer his expertise.

By that time more than 100 companies were licensed to build geodesic domes. By 1966 there were over 5,000 such structures in 50 countries and just six years later there were more than 50,000 domes in existence. Fuller's masterpiece was the 200-foot high, 250-foot diameter United States Pavilion which awed visitors at Montreal's Expo '67. The structure was covered with separate panels, connected to a battery of 250 electric motors, that could open or close to keep the building at a comfortable temperature.

But even though his masterful idea earned him fame and fortune, Fuller's vision of the mass-produced dome house has never come close to being fulfilled. Thirty years after Buckminster Fuller received raves for his architectural wonder, domes are still a rarity. Sure, there are people who build them, but most of those people are rugged individualists who don't mind bucking established ways of doing things. Majestic domes that overwhelm the senses with their detailed and delicate patterns are put up now and again for people to gape at, but they are still considered quite exotic. Novel ideas such as home computers, Jacuzzis, water beds, microwave ovens, and even "pet rocks" have gained acceptance, while Fuller's mass-produced dwellings of the future go largely unnoticed. The customs of the building industries, rooted in place for so long, are still difficult to budge.

A dome over the Religious Center at Southern Illinois University at Edwardsville, Illinois. Blue plexiglass represents the waters of the earth, and clear plexiglass represents the continents. The map places Edwardsville exactly at the top of the dome.

A modern geodesic dome home.

Looking up through the dome at Edwardsville.

The dome at Montreal's Expo '67. It is now part of "Man and His World," a theme park in Montreal.

3
IDEAS TO SAVE THE WORLD

Machines to Make Us Rich

If Buckminster Fuller didn't have command of the architectural world, at least he had won its respect. In fact, among many younger students who shared his idealism and sympathized with his battles against the establishment, Fuller became a hero. The squat, little man was looked up to as an example of someone who had fought against modern society and had at least won a battle or two.

There is a shock to almost all his proposals, and it is only after reflection that one concedes that yes, ultimately, or possibly in the not too distant future, it may indeed be so.
—*Isamu Noguchi, sculptor*

Bucky in front of the Dymaxion Map, talking, as usual.

Typically, though, Bucky was so busy charting his own course that he didn't fit neatly into the role of rebel. While many idealists spoke out for a simpler future, preached a back-to-nature lifestyle, and warned of the dangers of relying on technology to solve our problems, Fuller took the other side. To him machines and technological progress were not evil; they were going to make everyone in the world rich beyond their wildest dreams.

To many people, machines are cold, impersonal monsters that always have some nagging defects and always break down when you need them the most. Bucky's love of machinery, however, was so great that it once spoiled what was supposed to have been a harsh punishment. After wasting all his money and getting kicked out of Harvard before World War I, Fuller had been forced to face the wrath, not only of his mother, but of the entire collection of close-knit Fuller relatives. An urgent family conference was called and it was decided that Bucky should be packed off to Quebec, Canada, to work in a cotton mill owned by one of the Fullers. There Bucky was supposed to have gotten a taste of the sweaty, boring work of an unskilled laborer. The idea was that Bucky would be so frightened at the prospect of working like that all his life that he would understand the value of studying hard in order to get a good job.

One little hitch came up, though, that no one in the family could have predicted. Bucky *enjoyed* working in the mill, far better than he had liked being at Harvard. He marveled at the machinery, and traced in his mind the ideas that led to the creation of these fascinating inventions. So enthusiastic was Fuller in his work with these cotton mill machines that his family wrongly concluded that their plan had worked. They supposed that Bucky had finally come to his senses and developed good work habits, and that he was trying hard to prove that he had learned his lesson. Proudly, they welcomed young Fuller back to Massachusetts and another try at Harvard. Bucky, however, found Harvard no more stimulating than before, and within a few months he completely baffled his family by getting kicked out a second time.

Energy Slaves

Buckminster never lost his appreciation of what mechanical inventions could do. It was obvious to him that the key to getting more with less in the world was to build more and better machines to do more and better work. Fuller also discovered the key ingredient for operating a society of more and better machines, nearly 40 years before an Arab oil embargo proved he was right. In the 1930s, at a time when oil and gasoline were so cheap that it was easier to waste it than to conserve it, Fuller pointed out that it was really energy and not gold that determined the wealth of a society.

Below and right: **Energy slaves at work. If wheat was still harvested only by hand and goods moved only in amounts one man could carry at a time, we would live very different lives.**

In order to get his energy ideas across, Bucky used the concept of an *energy slave.* This term described the amount of work done by an energy-driven machine that equaled the amount of work that a person could do in the same amount of time. (Since machines are not paid for their work, Fuller used the term slave.) Bucky calculated that in 1972 each person on Earth was making use of an average of 200 energy slaves. In other words, if all machines were thrown out, we would need 200 hard-working slaves for every person on earth to keep our lifestyles the way they were in 1972. Of course, those energy slaves were not evenly spread out through the world. Fuller insisted that it was nothing but the lack of harnessed energy that kept the Third World nations from a lifestyle equal to that of the United States.

Energy experts today would not argue with that reasoning. But Fuller seldom liked to stop at what most people would consider reasonable. He went on to say that by increasing our use of energy slaves, we should be able to take care of every physical need of every person in the world. His argument was a simple equation: wealth = energy + knowledge. Since the amount of energy in the universe remains the same and cannot be destroyed or lost, that number in the equation will never decrease. At the same time, new discoveries continually add to the world's previous body of knowledge and make that part of the equation increase. Therefore, the world's wealth will always increase. All that remained in question was,

how soon do we want to bring about a utopia on earth? It was Fuller's contention that human beings are in a position to do whatever they want. Total success for humanity is possible.

Domed Cities and Floating Pyramids

With that optimistic view of the future, Fuller let his imagination go. How could he best change the environment so that it allowed humans a better life? Well, if it's possible to build domes over rooms, courtyards, and sports arenas, why not domes over entire cities? Who but Buckminster Fuller would not only dream such things, but calculate the cost and the benefits? He suggested that a dome two miles in diameter over Manhattan, New York, would make the city 50 times more energy-efficient. It would be much less wasteful to air-condition the whole city in a climate-controlled dome than to separately air-condition rooms and buildings the way it is done now. The savings in snow removal costs alone would pay for the dome in 10 years. Thanks to Fuller's designs, the people in the city wouldn't even know they were "inside." Bucky's dome required so little material in order to be strong that, with a transparent skin stretched over the framework, sunlight could still be enjoyed and the only visible effect of the dome would be a slight

An artist's rendering of Fuller's domed New York City.

darkening of the sky. Lack of rain would be no problem. Fuller proposed designing grooves into the dome that could collect rain water for the city's use.

Having made houses that could be mobile, Bucky went on to plan entire cities that did not need to be anchored to any property. One of

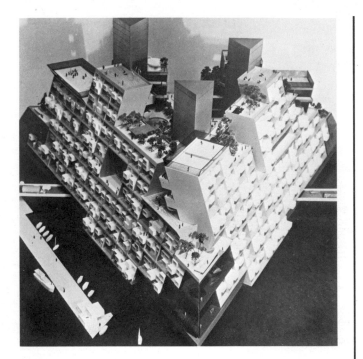

A model of the floating city. The apartments, like building blocks, could be detached from this city and plugged into a different one.

his ideas was a floating city, in the shape of a tetrahedron two miles long on each edge. This shape could stand up to earthquakes and hurricanes. Atomic reactors, cooled in the ocean water, would provide all the power, including energy to run the desalinization plants that would provide drinking water.

Spaceship Earth

Machines, atomic reactors, mastering the environment, meeting all human needs through technology and planning—from the sound of that, Buckminster Fuller could have been an oil company president or a big business lobbyist. Yet during his years as a researcher at Southern Illinois University in the 1960s, Bucky was a hero to the other side, the anti-establishment, counter-culture people. How did he cross the line that separated big industry from the back-to-nature crowd?

It's probably a question that Fuller would not have answered, because, continually breaking away from accepted patterns, he saw no reason why one couldn't believe in both sides. But perhaps a clue can be found in a conversation with an uncle during Bucky's younger days. This uncle called the boy aside to give him some advice on planning his future. He reminded Bucky that only one out of a hundred people in the world enjoyed the benefits and luxuries that he did. The only way that a young person could guarantee that he would enjoy those benefits was to make sure that those other 99 didn't. All that talk about charity and cooperation didn't mean a thing. It was you against the world and success had to be gained at the expense of others.

That short conversation must have gnawed at Bucky because over seventy years later he could still recall the details vividly. His uncle's argument sounded logical, but there was something in it that struck young Fuller as wrong. On that day in 1927 when he debated suicide on the shores of Lake Michigan, Fuller found where his uncle had made his mistake.

Fuller in front of part of his library at his dome in Carbondale, Illinois.

"We all belong to the universe," Bucky decided. "We're all in this together." "Continuous man" was a term he used to describe his idea that all people should contribute to the future of the human race as well as to their own needs.

Fuller's philosophy of being a part of the universe led him to be one of the first to introduce the idea of ecology to the general public. There was no greater enemy of his "more with less" motto than waste. If Bucky wanted to depress himself, all he had to do was think of all the world's cars that were at that moment standing still at stoplights. Millions of engines were gulping energy, spewing out waste, and doing absolutely nothing worthwhile. As much as he liked machines and industry, Fuller pointed out that we can't act as if we can do anything we like to nature. Bucky used a new term that eventually became so popular it was used as a theme by Governor Jerry Brown, Democratic presidential candidate in 1976. Bucky illustrated our dependence on nature by calling our planet "Spaceship Earth." By that term he tried to show that there are limits to our world, that it is a closed system. We can't act as though there's an endless supply of every resource or as though we can produce tons of garbage, poisonous and otherwise, without trashing our home.

The idea of Spaceship Earth also showed that since all people on earth share this limited space, it is crucial that we work and plan together for our future. Fuller broke away from the establishment by blasting the governments of the world. "Man can do whatever he wants, yet he invests only in race suicide," Bucky fumed, referring to the billions of dollars the world spends on weapons. He believed that if that money was put into design science, everyone would have enough of everything and there would be no need to fight for anything.

World Citizen

Bucky included politics in his creative plans for the future. Considering it high praise that he was sometimes billed as "Buckminster Fuller, World Citizen," he dreamed of world citizenship for all. Advanced technology could link everyone to a computer system. Whenever an issue came up, everyone would punch in his or her vote, the computer would total the votes, and the issue would be decided. That was an example of the overwhelming faith Bucky had in people, a confidence that even many of his admirers did not share.

Fuller's invention called the "World Game" received a better reception. In this game, the players took inventory of the world's resources and needs and tried to come up with a plan to match the resources to the needs. The basic rule of the game was that no one wins

Bucky led sessions of the World Game while he was alive. The World Game Project still exists and is still putting together information on world resources and needs.

unless everyone wins. Bucky toyed with the idea of a massive, computerized version of the game that could go into great detail. But the expense was too great and he had to settle for smaller versions of the non-competitive contest.

A model of the full-scale World Game that Fuller hoped to build.

4

THE MAN BEHIND THE IDEAS

My ideas have undergone a process of emergence by emergency. When they are needed badly enough, they're accepted. So I just invent, then wait until man comes around to needing what I've invented.

—R.B.F.

Buckminster Fuller, World Citizen, Pied Piper of the Universe, died July 1, 1983, just short of his 88th birthday. Of all the mysteries about this unusual man, perhaps the greatest is, how did he last so long at the pace he kept? From the accounts of his friends, watching Fuller at work was something like watching a gymnast in action. Only this gymnast keeps spinning and leaping for hours without a break until the spectators are breathless, wondering when he will quit.

Fuller's lectures were as unpredictable as the man himself. Without planning what he would say, he would go out to meet the audience and start talking. Much of the time he was just thinking out loud and the thrill of new ideas popping into his brain got him so excited he couldn't stand still. After he took the advice of his second daughter Allegra that he stop being so stiff behind the lecture podium, Bucky would spin and flail his arms as he warmed to the topics that came to mind. Some of the time he wandered off into a technical language that few but he could understand, yet still managed to get his audience caught up in his enthusiasm. Even in his 80s, Fuller could go on for as long as four or five hours before giving up the stage. Then he would jet around to another part of the world to start the process all over again. He refused to slow down his pace, insisting that he needed to accomplish as much as he could in the short time that he had left.

The trait that was most obvious, even to those who did not know him personally, was his stubborn commitment. With his short, stocky build and strong shoulders, he even looked like that symbol of determination, the bulldog. As much as Buckminster believed that you change people by changing the environment, his own uncompromising life was evidence that at least a few hereditary traits are unchanged by time or surroundings. Fuller's stubborn independence seemed to have been passed on intact from his great-great-

Fuller speaking with Chinese engineer in Peking in 1977.

grandfather, who, as a delegate to the Federal Constitutional Assembly at the birth of this country, refused to vote for passage of the Constitution because it said nothing about excluding slavery from the country. That trait popped up again in Bucky's grandfather, who, although a non-combatant chaplain in the Civil War, took matters into his own hands when Union troops balked at crossing a bridge. Grandpa Fuller's suicidal charge across the bridge under murderous fire sounds very much like many of Bucky's later forays into the business world. After Buckminster Fuller decided that a person ought to drink plenty of fluids to keep healthy, there was no wavering from his routine of 40 to 50 cups of weak tea per day. If common terms in our language were not scientifically precise, Fuller refused to use them. You would never catch Bucky saying "up" or "down" because in the universe there is no such thing, only "in" and "out." If you mentioned that the wind was blowing from the north, Fuller would correct you by saying it was "sucking from the south."

Scientists, inventors, and philosophers often come across to the public as serious, unemotional creatures who are fairly dull to be around. Even the most careful reading of his life and all his ideas will give only a glimpse of the wild, witty character that was Buckminster Fuller. He was as comfortable making up silly songs or dressing up in ridiculous costumes as he was probing the secrets of the universe. Obviously, anyone who would choose a middle name of Buckminster over his first name of Richard didn't mind being the center of attention. Most who met him insisted that he was like many an amusing story or anecdote: you had to be there to really understand what he was about.

Was Buckminster Fuller a genius, the Leonardo da Vinci of the 20th century? Did he succeed in his self-appointed mission to save the world?

The world is still here, but the problems of poverty, injustice, and the threat of nuclear destruction remain as strong as ever. It is not necessary that Bucky was successful, or even correct in all of his ideas. The fact remains that he has left his mark upon the world. Ideas take time in order to work their changes and it may be that we haven't yet begun to see the results of Fuller's life. Even now we can say that the world is a little different and, arguably, a little better because Richard Buckminster Fuller saw the world differently from others. If not for Bucky, how long would it have been before someone asked a question like, "how much does a house weigh?"

Bucky Fuller, free spirit.

Bibliography

This partial bibliography lists books about and by Richard Buckminster Fuller. Bucky wrote everything from philosophy to mathematics to poetry, and most of his works are still available in libraries.

Books about Buckminster Fuller:

Hatch, Alden. *Buckminster Fuller: At Home in the Universe.* New York: Crown, 1974. Hatch uses a lifetime fund of friendship, begun when they met in 1915, and adds pertinent researched details to paint a lively picture of Fuller's life. Indexed.

Marks, Robert and R. Buckminster Fuller. *The Dymaxion World of Buckminster Fuller.* Garden City, New York: Anchor Press/Doubleday Books, 1973. A straightforward, factual account of Fuller's inventions and life, full of detail and including an appendix of illustrations which takes up two-thirds of the book. Interesting, enjoyable, and precise. Indexed.

Snyder, Robert. *R. Buckminster Fuller.* New York: St. Martin's Press, 1980. Combines Fuller's own comments with additional information supplied by the author and a great many illustrations to paint an impression of Bucky's life. Snyder married Fuller's daughter and thus had access to many private papers, anecdotes, and photographs.

Books by Buckminster Fuller:

Education Automation. Carbondale, Ill.: Southern Illinois University Press, 1963. Fuller's ideas on education come together in this suggested plan for a new educational system.

GRUNCH of Giants: Gross Universal Cash Heist. New York: St. Martin's Press, 1983. This is a look at the international giants which control the world economies and resources, and how they could better be directed toward saving humanity (producing livingry) than destroying it (producing weaponry).

Inventions: The Complete Patented Works of R. Buckminster Fuller. New York: St. Martin's Press, 1983. Illustrated. See Patents in resource list below.

No More Second Hand God. Carbondale, Ill.: Southern Illinois University Press, 1963. A collection of poems and essays, containing much of Fuller's philosophy and mathematical speculation.

Operating Manual for Spaceship Earth. Carbondale, Ill.: Southern Illinois University Press, 1969. Ideas about the relationship between mankind and the spaceship we ride through the Universe. Bucky looks at the history of power and knowledge, and the possible futures of the Earth and of mankind.

Synergetics: Explorations in the Geometry of Thinking. Vol. I. New York: Macmillan, 1975. *Vol II.* New York: Macmillan, 1979. With Edgar Applewhite. Together these two volumes contain an entirely new geometry (and way of looking at the world) which Fuller based on his observations of nature.

--- with Richard J. Brenneman, ed. *Fuller's Earth: A Day With Bucky & the Kids.* New York: St. Martin's Press, 1984.

--- and Anwar Dil. *Humans in Universe.* New York: Mouton, 1983. Illustrated. Essays of Fuller's and Dil's philosophy, covering such topics as world interdependence, global resources, and peace.

--- with William Marlin, ed. *Artifacts of R. Buckminster Fuller—A Comprehensive Collection of His Designs and Drawings: The Dymaxion Experiment, 1926-1943, Vol 1. Dymaxion Deployment, 1929-1946, Vol 2. Designs, 1947-1960, Vol 3. Designs, 1960-1983, Vol 4.* New York: Garland Publishing, 1984. The definitive collection of Fuller's designs and drawings.

Related Topics
and Sources of Information

These resources offer information on Fuller and on topics of interest to him. Kits, models, films, videotapes, games, maps, books, and newsletters are a few of the items you can obtain from them.

The Buckminster Fuller Institute. The purpose of the Institute is to see to it that Buckminster Fuller's work is made accessible, so that it can be further researched, developed, and applied toward humanity's success. The Institute is the custodian of the extensive Buckminster Fuller Archive. It also publishes a bi-monthly news bulletin, presents educational programs, and makes available a complete selection of books, maps, tapes, and other educational materials. For a free catalog, write to The Buckminster Fuller Institute, 1743 South La Cienega Blvd., Los Angeles, CA 90035, or call (213) 837-7710.

Earth Rescue Corps. This organization is involved in such activities as the World Problems Expo, an international gathering of peace, environmental, and other organizations to exchange information about world problems, international travel, and related topics. For information about the organization write Earth Rescue Corps, 1480 Hoyt Street, Suite 31, Lakewood, CO 80215.

U.S. Patent Office. Copies of Buckminster Fuller's patents can be obtained from the U.S. Patent Office. For each patent, specify the patent number you want, and send $1.50 (postage is included in the fee) to Commissioner of Patents and Trademarks, Box 9, Washington, D.C. 20231. You will receive copies of the explanations and diagrams Bucky submitted with his application.

Some patents that might be of interest:

Dymaxion map, 2,393,676;

Geodesic domes, 2,682,235;

Dymaxion bathroom, 2,220,482;

Dymaxion car, 2,101,057;

Dymaxion Deployment Unit (a dwelling using the same materials and basic shape as a grain silo), 2,343,764;

Paperboard geodesic domes, 2,861,717;

Octet truss, 2,986,241.

For a more complete listing of Bucky's patents, see *Inventions: The Patented Works of R. Buckminster Fuller* (New York: St. Martin's Press, 1983) by R. Buckminster Fuller. This includes copies of the original blueprints and patent applications for 28 of Bucky's inventions, including the Dymaxion house, the Dymaxion map and the geodesic dome.

The World Constitution and Parliament Association. Truly international in membership and concerns, the Association organizes sessions of the Provisional World Parliament. It is seeking ratification of the

Constitution for the Federation of Earth, and attempts to define world problems and priorities and set up world organizations to find solutions for them. Write World Constitution and Parliament Association, 1480 Hoyt Street, Suite 31, Lakewood, CO 80215.

The World Future Society. Publisher of a magazine called *The Futurist,* available to members, the Society is interested in humanity's future. The Society sponsors local chapters, offers books and gifts of interest to members, and organizes conferences and general assemblies. Write to The World Future Society, 4916 St. Elmo Avenue, Bethesda, MD 20814-9968 for information about current membership fees and activities.

The World Game Project. The game was originated by Buckminster Fuller "as a creative alternative to war games." Its goal, stated by Bucky, is "To make the world work/for 100% of humanity/in the shortest possible time/through spontaneous cooperation/without ecological offense/or the disadvantage of anyone." The organization describes itself as a computer game, a source of global information, and a planning tool. Its "World Game Workshops" directly involve the audience in planning for the future, and it offers items (such as films, books, and a newsletter) relating to the world, its resources, and our future. Write to The World Game Project, 3508 Market Street, Philadelphia, PA 19104 for more information.

Index

(Numbers in **bold** refer to photographs and drawings.)

Acknowledgements: The photographs in this book are reproduced through the courtesy of: Buckminster Fuller Institute, pp. 1, 13, 18, 20, 21, 45 (bottom), 46 (top), 63, 64; Southern Illinois University at Carbondale, pp. 6, 25 (both), 27, 33, 58-9, 65, 68; North Carolina Department of Cultural Resources, Division of Archives & History, pp. 9, 48, 49, 69, 71; AMARC, pp. 2-3, 7, 34, 57 (bottom), 69; Wide World, pp. 11, 70; Archives of the Minneapolis Institute of Art, p. 15 (bottom); Milton Academy, pp. 16-17 (bottom); North Carolina State University, p. 19; William F. Harrah Automobile Museum, p. 30 (center); Daystar Shelter Corporation, Blaine, MN, pp. 35, 47 (bottom), 52, 56 (bottom), 79; UPI/Bettmann Newsphotos, pp. 42, 55 (both); Ford Motor Company, p. 50; Mahoney/Wasserman & Associates for Hilton Hotels in Hawaii, p. 53; Quality Industries, Inc., p. 54 (top); Union Tank Car Company, p. 54 (bottom); Southern Illinois University at Edwardsville, pp. 56 (top), 57 (top); U.S. Department of Agriculture, p. 60; City of New York, p. 61; World Game Project, p. 67; Library of Congress, pp. 40, 80; National Archives, pp. 12, 22-23.

Illustrations from patents of inventions, courtesy of the Commissioner of Patents & Trademarks: pp. 14, 15, 16, 38, Patent #2,986,241; p. 22, Patent #3,524,422; pp. 29, 30, 31, Patent #2,101,057; p. 36, Patent #1,604,097; pp. 40, 41, Patent #2,343,764; pp. 44 (top), 46, 47, 51, Patent #2,682,235